BILINGUAL SONGS

English-Spanish vol. 4

by
Diana Isaza Shelton
Music by Sara Jordan

Produced and Published by
Sara Jordan Publishing
a division of ℗©2005 Jordan Music Productions Inc.
(SOCAN)

ISBN 978-1-55386-038-9

Acknowledgments / Reconocimientos

Author - Diana Isaza Shelton

Editors - Mariana Aldave, Robert Gaiero, France Gobeil

Composer and Producer - Sara Jordan

Music Co-producer, Arranger, Engineer - Mark Shannon

Male Singer - Ricky Franco

Female Singers - Laura Azahar, Jennifer Moore, María Pérez

Illustrations - Jessica Jordan-Brough

Cover Design - Campbell Creative Services

Interior Layout - Darryl Taylor

Digitally Recorded and Mixed by Mark Shannon,
The TreeFort, Toronto, Ontario, 2005.

For further information contact:

Jordan Music Productions Inc.
M.P.O. Box 490
Niagara Falls, NY
U.S.A. 14302-0490

Jordan Music Productions Inc.
R.P.O. Lakeport, Box 28105
St. Catharines, Ontario
Canada, L2N 7P8

Internet: www.SongsThatTeach.com
E-mail: sjordan@sara-jordan.com
Telephone: 1-800-567-7733

Dedicated to all those who pursue the acquisition of language proficiency for knowledge and pleasure.

Dedicado a todas aquellas personas, quienes se esfuerzan por adquirir destreza en un segundo idioma, por conocimiento y placer.

The translation of these bilingual songs is close in most cases, however, in some verses similar words and phrases were used to obtain better musical results.

We acknowledge the financial support of the Government of Canada through the Book Publishing Industry Development Program (BPIDP) for our publishing activities.

Contents/Contenido

Hints for Teachers

and Parents

Bilingual Songs: English-Spanish, vol. 4, has been developed for use by second language learners, instructors, parents and teachers.

These songs, featuring curriculum based content, offer an attractive and easy-to-use format that facilitates learning in both Spanish and English.

Complying with the five major principles of the Standards of Foreign Language Learning: *Communication, Culture, Connections, Comparisons,* and *Communities*, these bilingual songs integrate skill development through exciting rhythms and melodies that also provide a real-world context for cultural understanding.

Students will improve literacy, vocabulary, reading, and comprehension skills through the rules and examples in this lyrics book. This program works well for learners with diverse learning styles, backgrounds, and disciplines at the beginning level. The lessons can be carried into many areas of study, and more importantly, go beyond the classroom and become part of students' lives at home and in the community.

Enjoy it! *¡Disfrútalo!*

This learning kit has three components: an audio CD, a 48 page lyrics book and an optional 64 page resource book. They can be used separately, however, if used in tandem, better results will be obtained.

All of the songs in this volume can be used to teach either Spanish or English. The bonus instrumental tracks, which are included on the CD, further boost language fluency as students use the lyrics book to perform "karaoke" style.

A few ways to use this resource:

This resource works well as both a remedial tutorial and as an enriching curriculum supplement.

In the classroom:

- ☑ Have beginning students listen while using the lyrics book. Later, have them sing along.

- ☑ Encourage confident students to perform "karaoke style" with the music accompaniment tracks.

- ☑ Advanced students may use the music tracks to create and perform original lyrics (boosting their writing skills).

- ☑ Employ the "cloze" method of learning by "whiting out" some of the words (using a photocopied sheet of lyrics) and have students fill in the words while listening.

At home or in the car:

- ☑ Whether you listen on the family stereo, through a stereo headset, or in the car, *Bilingual Songs: English-Spanish, vol. 4* can be great fun and entertainment for the entire family.

Introduction
Introducción

chorus/*coro:*

Hey there, brothers. Come and join along!
Hey there, sisters. Celebrate in song.

> *Hola, hermanos. ¡Vengan todos ya!*
> *Hola, hermanas. Todos a cantar.*

Learning can be lots of fun
when each thing we learn is sung.
Soon we will learn much more
with 'Bilingual Songs, vol. 4'.

> *Aprender es divertido*
> *cuando cantas lo aprendido.*
> *Con 'Bilingual Songs, vol. 4'*
> *tú serás el mejor.*

chorus/*coro:*

'You'
'Tú' y 'Usted'

chorus/*coro:*

'You', 'you', 'you'.
In English, it's a simple 'you'.
'You', 'you', 'you'.
How are you today?

> 'You', 'you', 'you'.
> *En inglés simplemente* 'you'.
> 'You', 'you', 'you'.
> *¿Cómo está usted hoy?*

In Spanish there are many ways
that we can say 'you'.
Each situation dictates
the proper form we choose.

We use *'tú'* for a friend.
'Usted' shows respect.
'Ustedes', for a group.
We are not finished yet.

In countries where Castilian Spanish
is spoken, like Spain,
the plural forms for 'tú'
are 'vosotros' and 'vosotras'.

chorus/*coro:*

Si a alguien te vas a dirigir,
debes escoger
entre informal y formal,
según la situación.

Usa 'tú' con amigos,
'usted' con los demás,
'ustedes' cuando es grupal.
¡Espera que hay más!

En algunos países del mundo,
varía el español:
la forma plural de 'tú'
es 'vosotros' y 'vosotras'.

chorus/*coro*:

I'm 'Mr. Ruiz'.
You are my new students.
>*Yo soy el 'señor Ruiz'.*
>*Ustedes son mis nuevos alumnos.*

We'll have lots of fun.
But tell me first where you're from.
>*Nos divertiremos juntos.*
>*Digan ustedes de dónde son.*

I am Felipe, from Peru.
I am pleased to meet you.
>*Soy Felipe del Perú.*
>*¡Mucho gusto! ¿Y tú?*

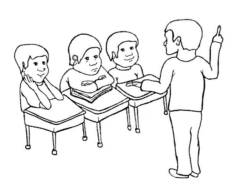

I am from Spain. My name is Raúl,
and who are all of you?
> *Soy de España. Me llamo Raúl.*
> *Y vosotros, ¿quiénes sois?*

I am from Egypt. I am Shatir,
and where are you from, teacher?
> *Soy de Egipto. Me llamo Shatir.*
> *Díganos profesor, ¿de dónde es usted?*

I am Mr. Ruiz, I'm from Mexico.
Class is over. Let's go.
> *Soy el señor Ruiz. Soy de México.*
> *Hemos terminado. Vámonos.*

chorus/*coro:*

Unisex Nouns
Los nombres unisex

chorus/*coro:*

'Round and 'round and 'round we go.
Some things change and some things don't.
In Spanish you must remember the gender.
You need to learn these things by rote.

> *Mira con mucha atención*
> *al género en español.*
> *Recuerda cuándo no hay que cambiarlo.*
> *Lo aprenderás con esta lección.*

Rap:

These nouns stay the same,
but the preceding articles change.
Veamos cuando la misma palabra usamos
y sólo el artículo cambiamos.

I'm a good cyclist.
 Soy un buen ciclista. (m)
I'm a good cyclist.
 Soy una buena ciclista. (f)

I'm a good student.
 Soy un buen estudiante. (m)
I'm a good student.
 Soy una buena estudiante. (f)

I'm a good journalist.
 Soy un buen periodista. (m)
I'm a good journalist.
 Soy una buena periodista. (f)

I'm a good tourist.
 Soy un buen turista. (m)
I'm a good tourist.
 Soy una buena turista. (f)

chorus/*coro:*

I'm the best artist.
   Soy el mejor artista. (m)
I'm the best artist.
   Soy la mejor artista. (f)

I'm the best astronaut.
   Soy el mejor astronauta. (m)
I'm the best astronaut.
   Soy la mejor astronauta. (f)

I'm the best athlete.
   Soy el mejor atleta. (m)
I'm the best athlete.
   Soy la mejor atleta. (f)

I'm the best guide.
   Soy el mejor guía. (m)
I'm the best guide.
   Soy la mejor guía. (f)

chorus/*coro:*

The Verb 'to be'
El verbo 'estar'

chorus/*coro*:

Some things about a language
can be very hard.
In English, it's 'contractions'.
In Spanish, it's 'estar'.

You can learn them quickly
when you sing along.
'Estar' and 'contractions'
seem simple with this song.

Hay cosas en los idiomas
duras de estudiar.
Del inglés: las 'contracciones'.
Del español: es 'estar'.

Si cantas con nosotros,
las podrás aprender.
'Estar' y las 'contracciones'
¡las vas a retener!

(Yo) estoy en la escuela.
I am at school.
I'm at school.

    (Tú) no estás en la escuela.
    You are not at school.
    You aren't at school.

Él está en el hospital.
He is at the hospital.
He's at the hospital.

    Ella no está en el hospital.
    She is not at the hospital.
    She isn't at the hospital.

Nosotras estamos en el café.
We are at the coffee shop.
We're at the coffee shop.

    Ellos no están en el café.
    They are not at the coffee shop.
    They aren't at the coffee shop.

*Words in parenthesis can be omitted in Spanish because the subject is understood once the verb is conjugated.

Nosotros estamos en el hotel.
We are at the hotel.
We're at the hotel.

Ellas no están en el hotel.
They are not at the hotel.
They aren't at the hotel.

chorus/*coro:*

Usted está en el teatro.
You are at the theatre.
You're at the theatre.

Ustedes no están en el teatro.
You are not at the theatre.
You aren't at the theatre.

Vosotros estáis en la playa.
You are at the beach.
You're at the beach.

Vosotras no estáis en la playa.
You are not at the beach.
You aren't at the beach.

El auto está en el garaje.
The car is in the garage.
It's in the garage.

La bici* no está en el garaje.
The bicycle is not in the garage.
It isn't in the garage.

**bici= short form for bicicleta (*bicycle)

chorus/*coro:*

Nº 5

Phone Numbers
Los números telefónicos

chorus/*coro:*

Thanks for calling.
I'm not home.
Leave your number
after the tone.

It's nice to hear
from all my friends.
I'll call you back
before the day ends.

*Muchas gracias
por llamar.
Deje su número
después de la señal.*

*A mis amigos
me gusta oír.
Los llamaré
antes de irme a dormir.*

Hi! It's Greg.
I'm going to be late.
9 1 5 - 3 0 2 8
(nine, one, five, three, zero, two, eight)

¡Hola! Soy Greg.
De tiempo voy corto.
9 15 30 28
(nueve, quince, treinta, veintiocho)

Call me. Suzy.
Waste no time.
9 2 3 - 5 0 8 9
(nine, two, three, five, zero, eight, nine)

¡Hola! Soy Suzy.
Llámame en breve.
9 23 50 89
(nueve, veintitrés, cincuenta,
ochenta y nueve)

Did you know?

It is common practice in many Spanish-speaking countries, when giving a phone number, to list a single digit followed by pairs of numbers.

---

chorus/*coro:*

Thanks for calling.
I'm not home.
Leave your number
after the tone.

It's nice to hear
from all my friends.
I'll call you back
before the day ends.

Muchas gracias
por llamar.
Deje su número
después de la señal.

A mis amigos
me gusta oír.
Los llamaré
antes de irme a dormir.

Hi! It's Ted.
Andrés is with me.
8 4 0 - 1 5 2 3
(eight, four, zero, one, five, two, three)

¡Hola! Soy Ted.
Estoy con Andrés.
8 40 15 23
(ocho, cuarenta, quince, veintitrés)

Hi! It's Rose.
What time are you free?
5 1 2 - 8 0 4 3
(five, one, two, eight, zero, four, three)

¡Hola! Soy Rose.
¿A qué hora vienes?
5 12 80 43
(cinco, doce, ochenta, cuarenta y tres)

chorus/*coro:*

Thanks for calling.
I'm not home.
Leave your number
after the tone.

It's nice to hear
from all my friends.
I'll call you back
before the day ends.

Muchas gracias
por llamar.
Deje su número
después de la señal.

A mis amigos
me gusta oír.
Los llamaré
antes de irme a dormir.

How Often..?
¿Con qué frecuencia..?

chorus/*coro:*

How often do you clean?
Do you do it frequently?
How often do you read
or go to see a good movie?

> *¿Cada cuánto tú limpias?*
> *¿Lo haces frecuentemente?*
> *¿Cada cuánto tú lees*
> *o películas vas a ver?*

"Adverbs of frequency"
Describe how often things occur.
"Adverbs of frequency":
they're easy words to learn.

> *"Los adverbios de frecuencia"*
> *dicen la frecuencia de una acción.*
> *"Los adverbios de frecuencia":*
> *¡mira qué colección!*

Rap:

Always	*siempre*
Usually	*normalmente*
Often	*a menudo*
Sometimes	*algunas veces*
Seldom	*raramente*
Rarely	*rara vez*
Never	*nunca*

I always wash my face.
I usually clean my place.

I often eat too fast.
I sometimes skip a class.

I seldom exercise.
I rarely criticize.

I never agonize.
How 'bout you?

Siempre me lavo la cara.
Normalmente limpio mi casa.

A menudo como rápido.
Algunas veces me escapo.

Raramente hago ejercicio,
y rara vez critico.

Nunca me preocupo.
¿Qué tal tú?

chorus/*coro:*

How often do you clean?
Do you do it frequently?
How often do you read
or go to see a good movie?

> *¿Cada cuánto tú limpias?*
> *¿Lo haces frecuentemente?*
> *¿Cada cuánto tú lees*
> *o películas vas a ver?*

"Adverbs of frequency"
describe how often things occur.
"Adverbs of frequency":
they're easy words to learn.

> *"Los adverbios de frecuencia"*
> *dicen la frecuencia de una acción.*
> *"Los adverbios de frecuencia":*
> *¡mira que colección!*

What is Recycling?
¿Qué es el reciclaje?

chorus / *coro:*

Do you know these 'question words'?
WH 'question words'?
Do you know these 'question words'?
They're a snap to use.

>   *¿Sabes cómo preguntar*
>   *o cómo obtener información?*
>   *Las palabras para interrogar*
>   *mucho te servirán.*

What, why, who, when, where, which.
We'll use these words as we sing
a song about recycling.

>   *Qué, por qué, quién, cuándo, dónde, cuál.*
>   *Cantemos todos al compás*
>   *y aprendamos a reciclar.*

chorus / *coro:*

WHAT is recycling?
It's when we reuse things;
saving things that won't decay
and using them in another way.

> *¿QUÉ es el reciclaje?*
> *Es reutilizar*
> *lo que podemos guardar*
> *y volver a usar.*

WHY should we recycle?
It affects us all.
Recycling is one solution
for the problem of pollution.

> *¿POR QUÉ reciclar?*
> *A todos nos afecta.*
> *Es una solución*
> *al problema de la polución.*

chorus/*coro:*

WHO should recycle?
We all should recycle;
you, me and everyone.
A healthy planet is more fun.

> *¿QUIÉN debe reciclar?*
> *Todos comprometidos;*
> *tú, yo y todo el mundo.*
> *¡Un planeta más limpio!*

WHEN should we recycle?
24/7.
If we recycle all the time,
Planet Earth will manage fine.

> *¿CUÁNDO debemos reciclar?*
> *En todo momento.*
> *Reciclando todo el tiempo*
> *el planeta estará contento.*

WHERE should we recycle?
Every place we stay.
At home and at school,
recycling is the only way.

> ¿DÓNDE debemos reciclar?
> En todo lugar.
> En la casa, en la escuela,
> es la única manera.

WHICH things can we recycle?
Paper, metal, glass.
Plastic, too. Reduce trash.
If you're confused, be sure to ask.

> ¿CUÁLES cosas se reciclan?
> Papel, metal, vidrio
> y plástico... en cada sitio.
> ¡Si no lo sabes, pregunta!

chorus/*coro:*

How Much? How Many?
¿Cuánto(s)? ¿Cuánta(s)?

chorus/*coro:*

A little of this. A little of that.
Being the chef is a treat.
A little of this. A little of that.
I'll make so much to eat.

> *Un poco de esto. Un poco de eso.*
> *Ser chef es un placer.*
> *Un poco de esto. Un poco de eso.*
> *Vamos a comer bien.*

"How much?" "How many?"
Question words of quantity.
"How much?" "How many?"
These are words we use.

> *¿Cuánto? y ¿cuántos?*
> *preguntan cantidad,*
> *¿cuánta? y ¿cuántas?*
> *a la hora de contar.*

How much cheese will I use?
How many eggs to choose?
How much sugar do I need?
So many guests to feed.

¿Cuánto queso usaré?
¿Cuántos huevos pondré?
¿Cuánto azúcar agregaré?
Muchos van a comer.

chorus/*coro:*

How much milk will I use?
How many nuts to choose?
How much flour do I need?
So many guests to feed.

¿Cuánta leche usaré?
¿Cuántas nueces pondré?
¿Cuánta harina agregaré?
Muchos van a comer.

chorus/*coro:*

Pen Pals / Amigos por correspondencia

chorus/coro:

Hello, pen pal.
What do you say?
I'm pleased to write
to you today.

Let me tell you
a bit about me,
my appearance
and personality.

*Hola amiga
te quise escribir
para saludarte
y saber de ti.*

*Un poquito
te voy a contar
de mi apariencia
y personalidad.*

I'm hardworking.
I'm not lazy.
Sometimes my sister
drives me crazy.

She thinks she's shy
but she's not.
She's outgoing
and she talks a lot.

*Soy un buen
trabajador.
Mi hermana en casa
me vuelve loco.*

*Ella no es
tímida,
es extrovertida
y habla mucho.*

I have curly
dark brown hair.
My eyes are blue.
My skin is fair.

I'm not short.
I am tall.
I love to have fun
playing football.

*Pelo crespo
tengo yo,
ojos azules
y piel blanca.*

*No soy bajo.
Yo soy alto.
Me divierto
con el fútbol.*

chorus/*coro*:

Hello, pen pal.
What do you say?
I'm pleased to write
to you today.

Let me tell you
a bit about me,
my appearance
and personality.

Hola amigo
te quise escribir
para saludarte
y saber de ti.

Un poquito
te voy a contar
de mi apariencia
y personalidad.

I am short.
I'm not tall.
I don't like
football at all.

My hair is blonde.
My skin is dark.
I like playing frisbee
in the park.

Soy baja.
No soy alta.
Jugar fútbol
¡me espanta!

De pelo rubio
y piel morena.
Juego al frisbee
en la arena.

I am cheerful.
I'm not boring.
My obnoxious brother's
another story.

He thinks he's weak
but he's strong.
He's at the gym
all day long.

Soy alegre.
No me aburro.
Tengo un hermano
testarudo.

Cree ser débil
pero es fuerte.
Va al gimnasio
frecuentemente.

Hello, pen pal.
What do you say?
I'm pleased to write
to you today.

Hola amigo
te quise escribir
para saludarte
y saber de ti.

My Car
Mi auto

My car is big.
It's bigger than your car.
My car is fast.
It's faster than your car... by far.

> *Mi auto es grande,*
> *más grande que tu auto.*
> *Mi auto es rápido,*
> *más rápido que el tuyo... ¡mucho más!*

My car is sleek.
It's sleeker than your car.
My car's expensive,
more expensive than your car... by far.

> *Mi auto es fino,*
> *más fino que tu auto.*
> *Mi auto es costoso,*
> *más costoso que el tuyo... ¡mucho más!*

chorus/*coro:*

Bigger, faster,
newer, sleeker.
People say
my car's 'a keeper'.

More expensive,
more efficient.
My car's hot
and your car isn't... by far.

> *Más fino, nuevo*
> *y seguro*
> *dicen que*
> *es todo un tesoro.*
> *Más costoso*
> *y eficaz*
> *que el tuyo.*
> *El mío es mucho más... ¡mucho más!*

My car is new.
It's newer than your car.
My car's more efficient,
more efficient than your car... by far.

> *Mi auto es nuevo,*
> *más nuevo que tu auto.*
> *Mi auto es eficaz*
> *más eficaz que el tuyo... ¡mucho más!*

My car is clean.
It's cleaner than your car.
My car is fancy.
It's fancier than your car... by far.

Mi auto está limpio,
más limpio que tu auto.
Mi auto es fantástico,
es súper fantástico... ¡mucho más!

chorus/*coro*:

Hey! Wait a minute.
Hold on guy.
My ego's not hurtin'.
I'll tell you why.

You're not for real.
You're all talk.
Your silly car came
from a cereal box!... A toy car!

¡Oye! Espera,
¡no presumas más!
Mi ego no afectas.
¡No todo es verdad!

Tú no eres sincero.
Te gusta mostrar.
¡Ese súper auto
viene entre un cereal!... ¡y no es real!

chorus/*coro*:

Superlatives!
¡Los superlativos!

chorus/*coro*:

Superlative adjectives;
we use them when we compare things.
Superlative adjectives;
when we've three things or more.

> *Usa los superlativos*
> *cuando algo quieres comparar;*
> *con adverbios o adjetivos*
> *y si tienes tres o más.*

Fastest, tallest,
biggest, smallest,
weakest, finest.
So many we can learn.

> *El más rápido, el más alto,*
> *el más grande, el más pequeño,*
> *el más débil, el más fino,*
> *son superlativos.*

chorus/*coro:*

He is strong.
She is stronger,
but their cousin
is the strongest.

Your hair's long.
His is longer.
That kid, there,
has the longest.

Él es fuerte,
ella lo es más;
pero el primo
es el más fuerte.

Largo tienen
el pelo,
pero el de aquél
es el más largo.

chorus/*coro:*

His dog's small.
Hers is smaller,
but my puppy
is the smallest.

His mom's tall.
My mom's taller,
but their mom
is the tallest.

> *Chicos son*
> *sus perros,*
> *pero el mío es*
> *el más chico.*

> *Altas son*
> *sus mamás,*
> *pero la de ellos es*
> *la más alta.*

chorus/*coro:*

My Two Cents Worth
Dos centavos

chorus/*coro:*

Whether it's a statement,
exclamation, or a question,
the important thing in Spanish is
...the inflection.

> *No importa si es pregunta,*
> *exclamación o afirmación.*
> *Lo importante en español es*
> *...la entonación.*

Just the other day
I bought some lunch
and then I stopped to pay.
    "How much money
    do you have?"
            "Two cents."
    "Two cents?"
            "Yes...Two cents!"

Hace algunos días
compre mi almuerzo
y lo fui a pagar.

"¿Cuánto tiene usted, señor?"
    "Dos centavos."
"¿Dos centavos?"
    "¡Sí!...¡dos centavos!"

chorus/*coro:*

Just the other day
I bought some books
and then I stopped to pay.
    "How much money
    do you have?"
        "Two cents."
"Two cents?"
        "Yes...Two cents!"

Hace algunos días
compre dos libros
y los fui a pagar.
    "¿Cuánto tiene usted, señor?"
        "Dos centavos."
"¿Dos centavos?"
        "¡Sí!...¡dos centavos!"

chorus/*coro:*

Ask your retailer about other excellent audio programs by teacher, Sara Jordan

Bilingual Preschool™

These bilingual songs and games include I Spy, Follow the Leader and Mind Your Manners. This kit teaches: names of animals, counting, directions, polite expressions, places in the community, and counting (cardinal and ordinal numbers). Sung by native speakers, these bilingual songs are a perfect introduction to the new language. ENGLISH-SPANISH and ENGLISH-FRENCH

Bilingual Beginners

Upbeat songs, combined with reproducible lessons and activities, provide a firm foundation for beginners by teaching: greetings, alphabet, counting to 12, about vowels, consonants, telling time, animals, food, parts of the body, family members, colors, and much more! ENGLISH-SPANISH and ENGLISH-FRENCH

Bilingual Songs™ Volumes 1-4

*** Parents' Choice Award Winner! ***

This series teaches the basic alphabet, counting to 100, days of the week, months of the year, colors, food, animals, parts of the body, clothing, family members, emotions, places in the community and the countryside, measurement, opposites, greetings, gender, articles, plural forms of nouns, adjectives, pronouns, adverbs of frequency, question words and much more! ENGLISH-SPANISH and ENGLISH-FRENCH

Songs and Activities for Early Learners™

Dynamic songs teach the alphabet, counting, parts of the body, members of the family, colors, shapes, fruit and more. Helps students of all ages to learn basic vocabulary easily. The kit includes a lyrics book with activities which teachers may reproduce for their classes.
IN ENGLISH, FRENCH OR SPANISH

Thematic Songs for Learning Language™

Delightful collection of songs and activities teaching salutations, rooms of the house, pets, meals, food and silverware, transportation, communication, parts of the body, clothing, weather and prepositions. Great for ESL classes. The kit includes a lyrics book with activities which teachers may reproduce for their classes.
IN ENGLISH, FRENCH OR SPANISH

Math Resource/Lyrics Books with Audio CDs

Songs, group activities and reproducible exercises teach addition, subtraction, multiplication and division. The upbeat songs make learning memorable. The reproducible exercises reinforce what has been learned in the songs while also incorporating strands of the Common Core Math Curriculum.
IN ENGLISH, FRENCH OR SPANISH

Reading Readiness™ Songs

Packaged with a lyrics book which includes helpful hints for parents and teachers. This great introduction to reading uses both phonetic and whole language approaches. Topics covered include the alphabet, vowels, consonants, telling time, days of the week, seasons, the environment and more!
VERSIONS IN ENGLISH, FRENCH OR SPANISH

Grammar Grooves vol.1™

Ten songs that teach about nouns, pronouns, adjectives, verbs, tenses, adverbs and punctuation. Activities and puzzles, which may be reproduced, are included in the lyrics book to help reinforce learning even further. A complement of music tracks to the 10 songs is included for karaoke performances. Also great for music night productions.
IN ENGLISH, FRENCH OR SPANISH

Singing Sight Words Volumes 1-4

This collection of fun songs builds a solid foundation for all beginning readers. By incorporating Dolch sight words into memorable and catchy melodies, early readers are quickly able to recognize the more common and basic words found in age-appropriate literature. IN ENGLISH

Funky Phonics®: Learn to Read Volumes 1-4

Blending the best in educational research and practice, Sara Jordan's four part series provides students with the strategies needed to decode words through rhyming, blending and segmenting. Teachers and parents love the lessons while children will find the catchy, toe-tapping tunes fun.
IN ENGLISH

Lullabies Around the World

*** Parents' Choice Award Winner! ***

Traditional lullabies sung by native singers with translated verses in English. Multicultural activities are included in the lyrics book. Includes a complement of music tracks for class performances.
Pre-K - Grade 3 11 DIFFERENT LANGUAGES

Check out these great Resource Books full of reproducible activities and exercises for the classroom.

Bilingual Kids™ Volumes 1-4

Reproducible, black-line, thematic lessons and exercises, based on *Bilingual Songs*, teach the basic alphabet, counting to 100, days of the week, months of the year, colors, food, animals, parts of the body, clothing, family members, emotions, places in the community and the countryside, measurement, opposites, greetings, gender, articles, plural forms of nouns, adjectives, pronouns, adverbs of frequency, question words and much more! ENGLISH-SPANISH and ENGLISH-FRENCH

Spanish for Kids: Beginning Lessons

Reproducible, black-line, thematic lessons and exercises in Spanish, based on *Español para principiantes*, teach the alphabet, numbers, days of the week, opposites, colors, family members, body parts and much more! Lessons are enhanced with information about Hispanic culture. 64 pages. Beginner level. IN SPANISH

Spanish for Kids: Thematic Lessons

Reproducible, black-line, thematic lessons and exercises in Spanish, based on *Canciones temáticas*, teach common expressions, salutations, time, modes of transportation, pets, prepositions and much more! Lessons are enhanced with information on Hispanic culture. 64 pages. Beginner level. IN SPANISH

Please visit our English and Spanish websites, great meeting places for kids, teachers and parents on the Internet.

www.SongsThatTeach.com

www.AprendeCantando.com

For help finding a retailer near you contact Sara Jordan Publishing 1-800-567-7733